AF350176

STARTING & BUILDING A PROFITABLE BUSINESS: A MANUAL GUIDE FOR ENTREPRENUERS

Munyaradzi Gumbo-Mberi

Published by Munyaradzi Gumbo-Mberi, 2024.

While every precaution has been taken in the preparation of this book, the publisher assumes no responsibility for errors or omissions, or for damages resulting from the use of the information contained herein.

STARTING & BUILDING A PROFITABLE BUSINESS: A MANUAL GUIDE FOR ENTREPRENUERS

First edition. August 1, 2024.

Copyright © 2024 Munyaradzi Gumbo-Mberi.

ISBN: 979-8227353146

Written by Munyaradzi Gumbo-Mberi.

Dedication

DEDICATION

To my late brother Muchengeti, who passed away at the tender age of 14 in the year 2000. If he were here today, he would be so proud of me for publishing my first book. ***Though you are gone, you are not forgotten. Rest in peace.***

To my husband and my two children, thank you for being my number one fans. Your encouragement and support, even when I come up with crazy ideas, keep me motivated. I draw my strength to keep dreaming from you, and I appreciate you immensely. When things do not go my way, you always find the right words to lift my spirits. You guys rock!

To my parents, thank you for raising me to be a strong woman through the word of God. SALUTE! To all my family members, friends, and clients, your support has been tremendous.

Thank you for believing in me and encouraging me to document this book. I could not have done it without you.

To my mentors and coaches, thank you for your pivotal role in my growth as a person and in business. Many of you checked on me frequently to see how I was progressing with this book. I am proud to have you in my circle.

To my Heavenly Father, I owe you my all. Thank you, God, for keeping me and enabling me to write this book so that I can share my knowledge with the world and encourage others. I am nothing without you, and this book means nothing if you are not in it. ***I am because You are.*** I love you, Lord.

To aspiring entrepreneurs, business owners, clients, and all who will read this book, may you be blessed, and may your lives be transformed for the better. Thank you for your unwavering support in championing my vision to impact lives and make a difference in this world.

STARTING & BUILDING A PROFITABLE BUSINESS

A MANUAL GUIDE FOR ENTREPRENEURS

MUNYARADZI GUMBO-MBERI

Copyright ©2024 @Munyaradzi Gumbo- Mberi
All rights reserved. No part of this book may be reproduced or transmitted in any form or by any means, electronic or mechanical, including photocopying, recording, or by any information storage and retrieval system, without permission in writing from the copyright owner.

ISBN: 978-0-7961-3674-9
Edited by Patience Sakutukwa
Cover Design by Lindani L. Thango
Layout by Patience Sakutukwa
Published by Lebogang Sewela

Unless otherwise Scripture and quotation are taken from KJV

Inspirational Qoute

*"Do the best you can until you know better.
Then when you know better, do better."*
-Maya Angelou

DEDICATION

To my late brother Muchengeti, who passed away at the tender age of 14 in the year 2000. If he were here today, he would be so proud of me for publishing my first book. ***Though you are gone, you are not forgotten. Rest in peace.***

To my husband and my two children, thank you for being my number one fans. Your encouragement and support, even when I come up with crazy ideas, keep me motivated. I draw my strength to keep dreaming from you, and I appreciate you immensely. When things do not go my way, you always find the right words to lift my spirits. You guys rock!

To my parents, thank you for raising me to be a strong woman through the word of God. SALUTE! To all my family members, friends, and clients, your support has been tremendous.

Thank you for believing in me and encouraging me to document this book. I could not have done it without you.

To my mentors and coaches, thank you for your pivotal role in my growth as a person and in business. Many of you checked on me frequently to see how I was progressing with this book. I am proud to have you in my circle.

To my Heavenly Father, I owe you my all. Thank you, God, for keeping me and enabling me to write this book so that I can share my knowledge with the world and encourage others. I am nothing without you, and this book means nothing if you are not in it. ***I am because You are.*** I love you, Lord.

To aspiring entrepreneurs, business owners, clients, and all who will read this book, may you be blessed, and may your lives be transformed for the better. Thank you for your unwavering support in championing my vision to impact lives and make a difference in this world.

ACKNOWLEDGEMENTS

I extend my heartfelt gratitude to all those who have supported and encouraged me throughout the journey of writing **"Starting and Building a Profitable Business."** Your unwavering belief in me has been a constant source of inspiration to my family, friends, and mentors. I am deeply thankful for your encouragement, guidance, and love.

I would also like to express my appreciation to the readers who have embraced my words with open hearts and minds. Your enthusiasm fuels my passion for writing and sharing the wisdom I have gained over the years.

Special thanks to everyone who contributed to the writing of this book; your invaluable assistance is greatly appreciated. Your expertise and dedication have been instrumental in bringing this project to fruition.

Above all, I am grateful to God for His abundant blessings, guidance, and grace. Without His divine presence and inspiration, this book would not have been possible.

FOREWORD

I

n a world where the path to success is often shrouded in uncertainty, it is a rare privilege to encounter a work that not only illuminates the way but also empowers the reader with practical wisdom and profound insights. *"Starting and Building a Profitable Business"* by Munyaradzi Gumbo-Mberi stands as a beacon for aspiring entrepreneurs and seasoned business owners alike. From the moment I first engaged with this book, I was struck by its authenticity and depth. The author masterfully weaves together personal anecdotes, time-tested strategies, and actionable advice, creating a tapestry of knowledge that is both accessible and transformative. This is not just a book about business; it is a journey into the heart of what it means to be an entrepreneur. Self-awareness is the cornerstone of this journey. The author begins by guiding readers through a process of introspection, encouraging them to delve deeply into their passions, strengths, and aspirations. This foundational step is critical, for it is only by understanding oneself that one can navigate the complexities of the business world with confidence and clarity.

The chapters that follow build upon this self-awareness, offering a comprehensive roadmap for starting and growing a successful business. Each page is imbued with rich experience and profound understanding of the entrepreneurial landscape. Insights into market research, business planning, and strategic execution are invaluable resources for anyone seeking to turn their business dreams into reality.

What sets this book apart is its emphasis on authenticity. In a market saturated with generic advice, the author's voice is refreshingly genuine. Her insights challenge readers to stay true to their values and to build businesses that reflect their unique vision and purpose. This approach not only fosters sustainable success but also ensures that the entrepreneurial journey is fulfilling and meaningful.

As you embark on the journey through these pages, prepare to be inspired, challenged, and equipped with the tools you need to succeed. The wisdom and guidance within will serve as a trusted companion, helping you to navigate the highs and lows of entrepreneurship with resilience and grace.

"Starting and Building a Profitable Business" is more than just a guide; it is a testament to the power of self-belief, perseverance, and the unwavering pursuit of one's dreams. It is with great pleasure and confidence that I recommend this book to anyone who aspires to create a thriving and impactful business.

May you find the inspiration and knowledge within these pages to embark on your entrepreneurial journey with courage and conviction.

PREFACE

I

n the dawn of the 21st century, the world of business has undergone a remarkable transformation. The digital age has brought forth an unprecedented wave of innovation, connectivity, and opportunity. With the advent of the internet, the global marketplace has become more accessible than ever before, offering a vast array of resources and tools to aspiring entrepreneurs. Yet, despite this abundance of opportunities, many find themselves adrift in a sea of information, struggling to harness the full potential of these advancements. In today's hyper-connected world, we are bombarded with ideas and possibilities at every turn. Social media platforms, online marketplaces, and digital tools provide us with the means to turn our dreams into reality. However, the challenge lies not in the scarcity of opportunities but in the ability to navigate and utilize them effectively.

Many of us have access to the internet, a treasure trove of knowledge and resources, but often find ourselves squandering precious time on distractions rather than leveraging it to build our futures. Similarly, we may possess abundant resources but lack the guidance and insight to employ them wisely.

This book is a testament to the power of self-awareness, perseverance, and the pursuit of one's true calling. It is a chronicle of my own journey—a journey marked by trials, tribulations, and ultimately, triumph. When I first embarked on my entrepreneurial path, I faced numerous challenges and setbacks. I found myself inundated with advice and opinions, often feeling overwhelmed and confused about which direction to take. It was during these tumultuous times that I realized the importance of self-awareness and the need to understand my own strengths, passions, and limitations.

The process of starting my business was

not a straightforward one. I experienced moments of doubt and discouragement, confronted with the harsh realities of the competitive business landscape. However, it was through these experiences that I learned invaluable lessons and gained a deeper understanding of what it takes to succeed. I discovered that true success is not merely about having access to resources or opportunities, but about having the clarity and confidence to pursue one's vision with unwavering determination.

In writing this book, my aim is to share the insights and strategies that have been instrumental in my journey. I want to provide aspiring entrepreneurs with a roadmap that not only guides them through the practical aspects of starting and building a business but also helps them cultivate the self-awareness and resilience needed to thrive in the modern business world. This is not just a book about business; it is a guide to understanding oneself and navigating the complexities of entrepreneurship with purpose and passion.

I invite you to join me on this journey. Let us explore the myriad opportunities that lie before us, and learn how to harness them effectively. Together, we will delve into the heart of what it means to be an entrepreneur in today's world, and uncover the keys to building a successful and fulfilling business.

As you turn these pages, may you find the inspiration, knowledge, and courage to embark on your own entrepreneurial adventure. May you discover the power of self-awareness and the joy of pursuing your true calling. And may you, too, experience the triumph of turning your dreams into reality.

INTRODUCTION

B

eing an entrepreneur for several years has taught me the intricate art of building and operating a business from the ground up. My story is not one of instant success, but rather one of perseverance, resilience, and unwavering determination. I started my business with nothing but a dream and a fierce desire to succeed. Never in my wildest dreams did I imagine myself as a business owner. I was content working as an Accountant, believing that running a business was a privilege reserved for a select few, not for someone like me. But life has a way of pushing us toward our true potential.

At one point, I found myself in a toxic work environment that left me feeling overwhelmed and depressed. Coupled with ongoing health issues, I made the bold decision to resign without a backup plan. Sometimes the best way to go up in business or anything in life is becoming a bold risk taker. The thought of returning to the job market was agonizing, so I chose a different path—starting an accounting consultancy. This decision was driven by necessity and a lack of capital, as I planned to handle all the work myself. The fear of the unknown was daunting.

I had no idea where to begin and sought guidance from others in the business world, but time was a luxury they couldn't spare. Determined and with no other choice but to survive, I began piecing together information from the internet, social media, and any available resources. My partner supported me by buying a laptop when I had no savings left. With no clients initially, I taught myself to set up a Facebook page and boost posts. My first advertisement for company registration attracted five clients. Their satisfaction and referrals set my business in motion. I remember creating financial statements in Word format without any accounting software, a far cry from where I am now.

This journey inspired me to coach and motivate others who wanted to start their businesses. I began training groups because many couldn't afford one-on-one sessions. This book is a culmination of those teachings and my personal experiences. I believe that everyone has a unique talent or skill that can be transformed into a profitable business. When I first started, fear was my constant companion. Now, looking back, I realize how unfounded those fears were. Starting a business can be intimidating, but it is also incredibly rewarding.

Throughout my coaching and training, I encountered countless individuals who wanted to embark on their entrepreneurial journeys but were unsure of where to start or what they needed. This book addresses those concerns and provides a comprehensive guide on *"Where to start" and "How to start."* It is imperative that one ventures into business fully equipped and informed. We are in the era where it's easy to start a business but many are short sighted and do not calculate the costs well hence they gave up along the way or close down.

Building a business is not an overnight endeavor; it requires time, patience, and dedication. Many aspiring entrepreneurs dream of rapid success and substantial profits within a short period. However, true success lies in starting where you are with what you have and steadily working towards growth. Even the simplest ventures, like selling tomatoes, sweets, or ice cream, can evolve into substantial businesses with the right mindset and commitment. *"The best time to plant a tree was 20 years ago. The second-best time is now." – Chinese Proverb*

This book is designed to offer valuable insights and practical advice, whether you are a novice entrepreneur or a seasoned business owner. While many have written on this subject before, I am confident that by the time you finish this book, you will have a clear understanding of how to start and build a successful business.

Happy reading and may your entrepreneurial journey be filled with success and fulfillment!

Who
Am I!

CHAPTER 1

15

SELF-AWARENESS

"Knowing yourself is the beginning of all wisdom." — Aristotle

In the business world, many people project confidence and expertise, yet their outcomes often reveal a different story. Decisions made based on emotions or competition, without a clear understanding of costs or capacities, frequently lead to failure. Before embarking on any business venture, it is crucial to understand oneself, and this self-awareness remains essential throughout one's career and life.

Self-knowledge—being aware of one's character, feelings, motives, and desires—is often overlooked in both business education and daily life. *To make informed decisions, it is vital to deeply understand one's capabilities and limitations.* Self-awareness, as described by Travis Bradberry and Jean Greaves in "Emotional Intelligence 2.0," *involves deep personal honesty* and comes from *asking and answering hard questions.* This self-assessment is crucial in various areas of life, career, and business. Not every business suits everyone; specific character traits are necessary for success. This explains why some excel in certain ventures while others fail. An exceptional business idea may not always match the person attempting it. These questions are best answered through self-knowledge. Without it, one may become susceptible to every suggestion, leading to confusion.

People will always have something to say:

- *"So and so have failed; who do you think you are to succeed?"*
- *"No one will buy from you."*
- *"You should do this instead of that."*
- *"You don't have the required qualities."*
- *"This is not your type of business."*

- *"You will embarrass yourself."*
- *"I don't think you can do it."*

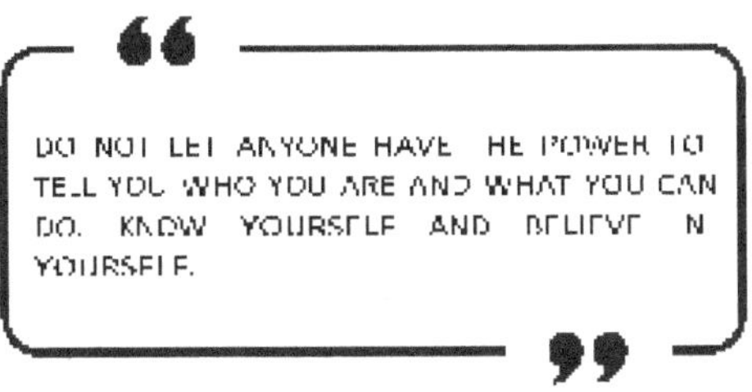

By understanding myself, I found the right path and avoided wasting time on unsuitable ventures. This self-awareness opened numerous opportunities, allowing me to discover and harness my talents and passions to build successful businesses. Without this self-understanding, I wouldn't be the business coach I am today. The power of knowing and understanding oneself is immense.

Tom Rath, in "StrengthsFinder 2.0," notes that the key to human development is building on who you already are. Self-awareness is foundational to building a profitable business. It enables individuals to make informed decisions, align their strengths with suitable business opportunities, and stand confidently in their choices. Embracing self-knowledge can transform not only your business journey but every aspect of your life.

Self-knowledge, the conscious awareness of one's character, feelings, motives, and desires, is often neglected in business teachings. To make informed decisions, one must deeply understand their capabilities and limitations. This self-assessment is vital in various areas of life, career, and business. Not every business suits everyone; specific character traits are necessary for success. An exceptional business idea may not always match the person attempting it. When I started my business, I lacked the self-awareness I have now. I pursued one venture after another and faced repeated failures. This is why I emphasize this topic; I went through that wilderness. Once I started understanding myself, I even laughed at some of my past business ideas. Out of ignorance, I wasted time on things I couldn't do.

Realizing the importance of self-awareness opened numerous opportunities for me. I discovered my talents and passions, which I utilized to build even more businesses. Without this exercise, I wouldn't be the business coach I am today. I never imagined I'd become a fluent public speaker. Understanding myself helped me cultivate hobbies that cope with daily challenges and stress. The power of knowing and understanding who you are is immense.

Self-awareness is a thorough assessment of who you are. It goes deeper than just your name. Knowing yourself is crucial in many areas of your life, career, and business. Not every business suits everyone; you need the right character traits. This is why some excel in certain ventures while others fail. An exceptional business idea might not match the person attempting it. For example, an introvert might struggle in a business that requires constant social interaction. We will explore how to do this self-assessment in five areas or categories that you need to analyze. Take this task seriously, as it will help you develop a better understanding of yourself and guide you toward the right business opportunities.

FIVE AREAS ANALYSIS TO TAKE

1. Passion

What drives you?
What do you love doing?
What motivates you?

1. Irritations

What irritates you?

What turns you off?

What discourages or hurts you?

What do you dislike?

1. **Weaknesses**

What are your weaknesses?

What is it that you don't like about yourself?

What do you want or wish to change about your behavior?

1. **Strengths**

What are your strengths?

What are you good at?

What do people compliment you about?

1. **Improvements**

Who do you want to become?

What do you want to acquire, or what skill do you want to have?

What behavior do you want to change or mold?

For instance, a business requiring extensive social interaction may not be suitable for an introvert, setting them up for failure. Accurate self-understanding simplifies decision-making in any situation. It empowers individuals to stand firm in their beliefs. Stephen R. Covey, in "The 7 Habits of Highly Effective People," emphasizes that *our behavior is a function of our decisions, not our conditions*. When starting a business, common questions include, *"What can I do?"* or *"Which products can I sell?"* Understanding your strengths, weaknesses, motivations, and values allows you to navigate the complexities of business with clarity and purpose. It is the compass that guides you through challenges and opportunities alike.

THE BENEFITS OF SELF-AWARENESS

> *Increased Confidence*: Knowing your strengths helps you work with confidence, as you're doing what suits you best.

> *Continuous Improvement:* Identifying areas for growth allows you to focus on and improve your weaknesses.

> *Motivation:* Doing what you love inspires you to continually improve and achieve more.

> *Resilience:* Self-knowledge makes you less affected by others' negative opinions, as you are grounded in your self-belief.

> *Better Decision-Making*: Understanding your capabilities leads to practical and informed decisions.

> *Control:* Clarity about yourself gives you a sense of control over your actions and decisions.

> *Clear Goals:* Self-awareness helps you set clear, achievable goals and understand the results you aim for.

> *Direction:* Knowing yourself provides a clear perspective on where you want to go in life and business.

> *Happiness and Satisfaction:* Engaging in activities you love brings joy and fulfillment.

> *Productivity and Results*: Focusing on self-improvement increases productivity and yields better outcomes.

> *Higher Success Rate:* Businesses founded on the owner's passions and strengths have a higher chance of success.

THE SELF-AWARENESS EXERCISE

Step-by-Step Guide:

1. *Get in a Good Mood:* Engage in an activity that you love and that helps you relax. This could be taking a walk, cooking your favorite meal, watching a show, running a bath, or reading a book. The goal is to put yourself in a positive space.

2. *Find a Quiet Place:* Go to a peaceful location with minimal noise where you can relax and reflect. Close your eyes as if meditating and let your mind wander.

3. *Write Freely:* Get a pen and paper and start writing anything that comes to mind. Don't overthink it; make it a fun exercise. Be honest with yourself—if you identify a weakness like *"jealousy,"* write it down without erasing it. Honesty is key to growth.

4. *Be Honest with Yourself:* No matter how small or uncomfortable an admission might be, write it down. This honesty will help you face and deal with your weaknesses, leading to personal growth.

5. *Seek Feedback:* Ask friends, family, and colleagues what they think about you as a person. Although it can be hard to hear about your weaknesses, find one or two people who will give you honest feedback. This will benefit you in the long run.

6. *Analyze Your Notes:* Review the information you've written down. Identify business ideas based on your passions and the things you love doing. Make a plan to address your weaknesses. Combine your strengths and passions to find the perfect business idea. Strategize on how to improve yourself and grow your business.

By following these steps, you can gain a deeper understanding of yourself, which is crucial for making informed decisions and finding the right business idea that aligns with your unique skills and passions.

IMPORTANCES OF SELF-AWARENESS

1. **Identifying Business Opportunities from Passions**:

Discovering what you love and enjoy doing can unveil potential business opportunities.

Examples of Passions: "You might find passion in baking, cooking, crafts, teaching, knitting, singing, sewing, decorating, and more."

Business Potential:

"Turning your passion into a business venture, such as starting a food business or running an Airbnb, can be fulfilling and profitable."

"For instance, my background in Interior Design helped me excel in managing my Airbnb, aligning my hobby with business success."

Focus and Growth:

"It's important to focus on one passion initially rather than spreading yourself too thin. As you grow, you can expand into other areas."

1. **Recognizing and Addressing Weaknesses**:

Understanding your weaknesses is crucial in assessing your suitability for specific business ventures.

Example: "You can have a passion for fashion, but if you lack confidence and grooming skills or dislike interacting with people, it may hinder your success."

Personal Consultation Experience:

"I once advised a lady in the fashion industry who struggled with confidence and presentation. Her initial reserved demeanor did not align with her business goals."

"Recognizing her potential, I encouraged her to attend business events, improve her appearance, and enhance her confidence through grooming courses."

Transformation Outcome:

"Today, she has grown significantly in her fashion business. Her renewed confidence and refined presentation have propelled her success."

The success or failure of a business idea often depends on aligning your skills, passion, and resources with the idea you pursue. An idea, in itself, is neutral—its outcome hinges on your ability to execute it effectively.

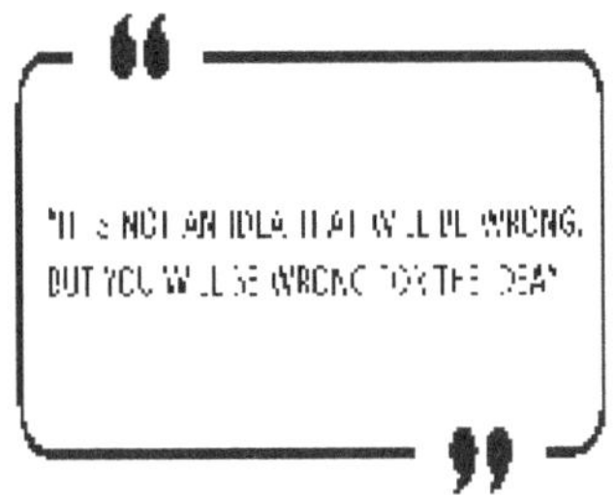

COMMON WEAKNESSES TO ADDRESS

- Anger issues
- Impatience
- Laziness
- Procrastination
- Jealousy
- Ungratefulness
- Lack of confidence
- Lack of focus
- Self-pity
- Poor communication skills
- Poor grooming, etc.

When you have listed the weaknesses or the characteristics that you don't want in your life anymore, go through each of them and see how you can work around them to improve yourself. Sometimes you need a professional to help you, or you can read books around it, or attend courses etc. What's most important is that you need to take action and not ignore your weaknesses because they will always drag you down.

IMPROVEMENT STRATEGIES

- "Identify and list the weaknesses or traits hindering your progress.
- Take proactive steps such as seeking professional help, reading relevant literature, or attending courses."

1. **Discovering and Capitalizing on Strengths:**
   - ***Self-awareness*** enables you to identify and leverage your strengths, crucial for personal and business success.
   - ***Personal Discovery:*** "Through self-awareness exercises, I uncovered strengths in teaching and motivational speaking, aligning my passion with my abilities."
     - ***"Utilizing strengths*** like excellent communication skills and a vibrant personality enhances your business effectiveness."
     - ***"Aligning passion*** with strengths often leads to successful ventures."

Some of the strengths that you can capitalise on are as follows:

-
-
-
-
-
-
-
-
-
-

- Patience
- Excellent communication skills
- Confidence
- Determined
- Focused
- People person
- Bubbly
- Fast learner
- Organized
- Attentive
- Disciplined

4. You can see the areas that you lack.

You realize that there is a certain strength or skill that you need, but that you do not have it yet. You should make it a point in your life to upgrade yourself and obtain the required skills you are missing.

Ways to gain a skill include:
-
- Enrolling in a course for that specific subject

Learning online via social networks.

Now there is a lot of e-learning happening all over internet platforms like YouTube, Facebook, LinkedIn and so on. You can also learn through cheaper channels like Udemy and other online platforms.

▪Reading books that cover that specific area of focus.

Self-awareness

Looking for a mentor or coach - someone in the field who can help you learn the ropes. *Always remember one rule: If you're too proud to ask, you will never learn.* Some people recognize their weaknesses and even know others in their field who could help them, but pride stops them from seeking assistance. Asking for help from experienced individuals can significantly shorten your learning curve and help you avoid costly mistakes.

In business and life, you can't know everything. Learning from and teaching others is essential—everyone has different strengths and weaknesses. This self-awareness exercise is designed to help you identify a business that fits you perfectly and understand where to focus your efforts. If your business is struggling, it might be because you need to improve in certain areas. For example, I know I'm not good at handling phone calls all day, especially managing many people over the phone. Understand your capabilities and limitations.

If you're already in business, identify areas that need improvement, cultivate new skills, and enhance your expertise. The key questions for aspiring entrepreneurs are:

- **Where do I start?** Begin by understanding yourself.
- **What can I do?** Discover your potential through the self-awareness exercise.

NEW MiNDSET
NEW RESULTS

CHAPTER 2

BUSINESS MINDSET

"You don't become what you want, you become what you believe."- Oprah Winfrey

A

business mindset is a collection of attitudes and beliefs that shape how you approach and handle business challenges. It involves the mental frameworks and perspectives that drive your decisions, actions, and reactions in the business world.

Cultivating a positive and proactive mindset is crucial because it influences your ability to seize opportunities, overcome obstacles, and achieve success. To build a profitable business, you need to change the way you think. One major obstacle is making excuses. We often fail to act on our desires because we create reasons why things are impossible. These excuses are rooted in limiting beliefs that can be changed with a shift in mindset. Consider Oprah Winfrey's words: *"You don't become what you want, you become what you believe."* This sentiment underscores a fundamental truth: your mindset shapes your reality. Here are some key points to address limiting beliefs and foster a positive mindset:

CHANGING BELIEFS

- ***Change Your Self-Talk:*** Drop the habit of complaining and adopt a positive outlook.
- ***Reject Victim Mentality:*** Stop feeling sorry for yourself and embrace confidence.
- ***Affirm Your Worth:*** Remind yourself of your value and potential.
- ***Believe in Success:*** Know that success is within your reach.
- ***Practice Gratitude:*** Focus on the good in your life and be

thankful.

A successful business mindset is characterized by:

- *Growth Orientation:* Belief in your ability to learn and adapt.
- *Resilience:* Capacity to bounce back from setbacks.
- *Vision:* Clarity about your goals and the future of your business.
- *Confidence:* Self-assurance in your skills and decisions.
- *Adaptability:* Willingness to embrace change and innovate.

OVERCOMING LIMITING BELIEFS

Many people hinder their progress by clinging to limiting beliefs:

- *Family Background:* Some believe that a disadvantaged background dictates future failure. However, many successful individuals come from humble beginnings and have reshaped their destinies.
- *Gender:* Gender barriers have diminished, and both men and women can excel in various fields. Success is not determined by gender but by drive and commitment.
- *Education:* Lack of formal education doesn't preclude business success. Passion, zeal, and a willingness to learn are often more critical.
- *Race:* Success is not restricted by race. Numerous successful entrepreneurs defy racial stereotypes and excel based on their abilities and determination.
- *Economic Environment:* Blaming the economy for business challenges can be a barrier. Many successful entrepreneurs thrive despite economic difficulties by adapting and innovating.

You must confront and dismantle these limiting beliefs to move forward. As you affirm your capabilities and practice gratitude, you can overcome obstacles and build a successful business.

Confront and dismantle these beliefs to move forward.

AFFIRMATIONS AND GRATITUDE

Affirmations are positive statements that help you challenge negative thoughts. Never accept a negative thought because it will cripple you. When it comes to your mind, you need to quickly distract yourself. Whenever you think of a business or wish to make certain decisions, fear can come creeping in. You start seeing failure, feeling as though you are not enough, and ultimately you start doubting that business idea. Don't tolerate such thoughts. It is okay to feel it, but what is not tolerable is to accept it. What has sustained me and is still sustaining me in my business today, is having a positive attitude, being grateful, not complaining and being hopeful.

Here is an example of positive business affirmations:

"I am worthy to run a successful business."

"I am smart and intelligent."

"I have so much energy and positivity."

"I do my business with so much confidence."

"I always have great ideas."

"My clients love me and refer my business to others."

"I offer a great service."

"I am good at what I do."

"I love my work."

Declare positive affirmations over your life every day and as many times as you want. When you say your affirmations, believe what you are saying, register them or impose them in your mind. If you are able to tune your mind, you have won. Let it believe what you want it to believe and trust me, things will start manifesting. Positive affirmations can be spoken over yourself, your business, or any situation. There will be times when you will be drained and feel like everything is going south, but when you start affirming yourself with conviction, the positive energy will come. I usually do this in front of the mirror at home.

Positive affirmations are just like prayers, declare them with faith and believe that whatever you say, is happening.

In the New Revised Standard Bible, the book of *Mark 11 verse 24,* says,

> *"So I tell you, whatever you ask for in prayer, believe*
> *that you have received it, and it will be yours."*

GRATITUDE

When you are grateful about something, that thing magnifies itself even further and you begin to see more and more of it in your life.

Be grateful, enjoy the little things; and be grateful for those small steps you make. If you are not grateful and all you do is just complain, the negative things that you are complaining about will also increase in magnitude. Practise gratitude, especially in the morning, as it sets the tone for the day. Having a grateful heart gives you energy whereas complaining on the other hand drains you and kills your morale.

What can you be grateful for?

-
-
-
- You are alive to offer a service or a product.

You have a business.

You have those few clients.

Your mind is sound.

Here is an example of a morning gratitude you can speak over your life and business:

"I am grateful that I am alive, fit, and in good health."

"I am grateful for this beautiful day."

"I am grateful for all my clients and the money I am getting today."

"I am grateful for my employees who help me."

"I am grateful for my suppliers who give me good service."

"I am grateful for the ideas that I have."

"I am grateful for my phone that works for me."

"I am grateful for my car that takes me from one point to another."

Just try it come up with a gratitude journal where you can write down all the things that you are grateful for every day.

WHAT TO AVOID

Don't let limiting beliefs hold you back:

1. "I am not good enough."
2. "I am cursed."
3. "It is for the selected few, not me."
4. "I am not educated enough."
5. "I am not smart or intelligent enough."
6. "I am not good-looking."
7. "I have no business connections."
8. "I come from a poor family."
9. "I have no capital."
10. "No one in my family has been successful, so I also can't."

Address these beliefs and affirm your capabilities. Remember, you are enough. Believe in your potential and start making a difference. Your greatness is inherent, regardless of background or limitations.

HOPE

"Hope is the only thing stronger than fear." — *Suzanne Collins*

Hope is the lifeblood of any successful business venture. In the face of challenges and setbacks, it is hope that often keeps the entrepreneur moving forward, believing in a brighter future. Without hope, many businesses would falter and cease to exist shortly after their inception.

The resilience and tenacity of entrepreneurs are largely fueled by their hope for improvement and growth. In the dynamic realm of business, hope serves as a beacon, guiding entrepreneurs through periods of adversity and uncertainty. It empowers them to face challenges head-on, to adapt to changing circumstances, and to persevere despite obstacles. This chapter explores the significance of hope in business and how it can be cultivated and maintained to ensure long-term success.

THE ROLE OF HOPE IN BUSINESS

Hope is not merely an abstract concept but a crucial element that sustains resilience and perseverance in the business world. It plays a pivotal role in motivating individuals to continue striving towards their goals, even when faced with difficulties.

According to research, hope has been shown to positively impact mental health and well-being, contributing to better problem-solving skills and increased motivation (Snyder, 2002). In my own experience with my Airbnb business, hope has been a driving force. Despite facing challenges such as property damage and difficult guests, maintaining hope has been essential.

It allows me to remain optimistic and focus on the potential for improvement. Hope fuels patience, enabling me to take each day as it comes while striving to enhance the guest experience and achieve better outcomes.

The COVID-19 pandemic stands as a powerful example of hope's impact. The pandemic caused significant disruption to businesses worldwide, yet hope was instrumental in their survival and adaptation. Businesses had to pivot their strategies, innovate, and persevere through unprecedented challenges. Hope was a critical factor in sustaining businesses and guiding them towards recovery. As the Bible says in Jeremiah 29:11, *"For I know the plans I have for you, declares the Lord, plans for welfare and not for evil, to give you a future and a hope."*

NURTURING HOPE

To cultivate and sustain hope in business, consider the following strategies:

1. ***Maintain Positivity:*** Focus on opportunities rather than setbacks. Research indicates that a positive outlook enhances problem-solving abilities and fosters resilience (Fredrickson, 2001). When faced with obstacles, maintaining a positive attitude helps you to see potential solutions and opportunities for growth.

2. ***Embrace Adaptability:*** Adaptability is key to overcoming challenges. Embracing change and viewing it as an opportunity for growth allows you to navigate the evolving business landscape effectively. According to the Harvard

Business Review, adaptable businesses are better positioned to thrive in uncertain environments (Tushman & O'Reilly, 1996).

3. ***Build Support Networks:*** Surround yourself with a supportive network of peers, mentors, and advisors. These connections provide encouragement, share valuable insights, and help you stay motivated during difficult times. Social support has been shown to enhance psychological resilience and foster hope (Cohen & Wills, 1985).

4. ***Practice Gratitude:*** Cultivate gratitude by acknowledging and celebrating small victories along your journey.

Gratitude enhances emotional well-being and helps maintain a positive outlook.

Keeping a gratitude journal can be a practical tool for focusing on the positive aspects of your business and life.

TRANSFORMING SETBACKS INTO OPPORTUNITIES

Hope is not just about wishful thinking; it involves actively transforming setbacks into opportunities. By fostering a hopeful mindset, entrepreneurs can turn challenges into stepping stones for success. Hope enables you to remain focused on your goals, adapt to changing circumstances, and persist through difficulties. Hope is a powerful force that anchors you amidst uncertainty and guides you toward a future filled with possibility.

By nurturing hope, maintaining positivity, embracing adaptability, building support networks, and practicing gratitude, you can enhance your resilience and perseverance in the business world. Remember, hope is not just a feeling but a driving force that propels you toward achieving your dreams.

Stop
making
excuses
and
make
moves

CHAPTER 3

38

OVERCOMING EXCUSES

"Success is not final, failure is not fatal: It is the courage to continue that count." – Winston Churchill

One of the biggest obstacles to turning business ideas into reality is the myth that success equals instant wealth. Many people believe that starting a business requires a huge amount of capital and that without it, their dreams are unattainable. However, entrepreneurship doesn't have to start with vast resources.

Many aspiring entrepreneurs are held back by excuses, with one of the most common being the misconception that success requires immediate wealth. People often think that starting a business demands substantial capital, but this isn't always the case (Hisrich, Peters, & Shepherd, 2017). In reality, entrepreneurship can begin with modest resources.Here's how to shift your mindset:

> **Start Small:** Entrepreneurship can begin with modest means. It's not about the amount of money you start with, but how you leverage your current skills and opportunities.

> **Incremental Growth:** Begin with a small venture, like selling everyday items. Success comes from consistent effort and gradually scaling up.

> **Utilize Skills:** Use your existing skills to minimize costs and handle tasks yourself, allowing you to start on a smaller budget.

OVERCOMING CAPITAL CONSTRAINTS

Capital constraints shouldn't deter you from pursuing your entrepreneurial dreams. Address financial limitations with the following strategies:

- **Start with What You Have:** Don't let a lack of capital stop you. Use available resources and reinvest profits to grow your business. Many successful startups began with minimal funding and relied on reinvested profits for growth.
- **Seek Additional Funding:** If more capital is needed, explore these questions:
    - How can I secure the necessary funds?
    - What are the prerequisites?
    - Where can I access funding?
    - What documentation is required?

For instance, the founders of Airbnb initially used their own savings and a small loan from friends to launch their platform, later seeking venture capital as they expanded.

OVERCOMING FEAR

Fear can paralyze potential entrepreneurs, preventing brilliant ideas from coming to fruition. Confront and overcome fear with the following strategies:

"Fear's Grasp and Hope's Light"

Fear, strong in its hold,
Darkens our dreams,
Stopping our goals and hopes.
But bravery, the cure for fear,
Pushes us ahead,
Bringing new ideas and success.

STRATEGIES TO OVERCOME FEAR

- **Acknowledge Fear:** Recognize that fear is a normal part of the entrepreneurial journey but should not dictate your actions. Embrace it as a natural part of growth.

- **Embrace Uncertainty:** Act despite fear. Often, the fear of failure is more daunting than the reality. For example, Elon Musk faced significant risks when starting SpaceX but moved forward with determination.

- **Learn from Others:** Successful entrepreneurs have also faced fears. Learn from their experiences and understand that acting despite uncertainties is often key to success.

FACING COMMON FEARS

1. **Starting Point Uncertainty:** Understand your strengths and passions. Begin with what you love rather than what others expect. For instance, Oprah Winfrey pursued her passion for media despite initial uncertainties.

2. **Expertise Apprehension:** Mastery comes through practice. Start at your current level, learn from mistakes, and improve continuously.

Steve Jobs started Apple with limited technical expertise but learned and grew along the way.

1. **Customer Acquisition Doubt:** Every business has customers. Differentiate yourself with integrity and excellent service. Companies like Zappos succeeded by focusing on exceptional customer service.

2. **Fear of Handling Success:** Plan for growth and strategize for

expansion. This proactive approach can help manage success effectively. For instance, Google developed a comprehensive growth strategy to handle its rapid expansion.

3. **Work-Life Balance Concerns:** Balance business and personal life by creating a routine that works for you. Seek support if needed. Richard Branson of Virgin Group emphasizes the importance of work-life balance in achieving long-term success.

4. **Fear of Failure:** Embrace failure as part of the learning process. Persist through setbacks and maintain a positive mindset.

5. **Procrastination:** Overcome procrastination by setting deadlines and holding yourself accountable. An accountability partner or mentor can provide additional support and motivation.

EMBRACING PATIENCE

Success in business rarely comes overnight. Patience is a key element:

- **Consistency:** Build trust and loyalty through consistent effort. Businesses like Starbucks achieved success through consistent quality and service.
- **Long-Term Vision:** Understand that business growth takes time and persistence. Companies such as Microsoft and Amazon illustrate the importance of maintaining a long-term vision.

Patience is essential for success. Just as a seed needs time to grow into a tree, your business requires time and consistent effort to flourish. Focus on long-term goals and remain patient; your hard work will eventually pay off.

By addressing excuses and obstacles with a strategic and resilient mindset, you can transform your business ideas into successful realities. Each challenge is an opportunity for growth. Embrace the journey with dedication and perseverance, and watch your entrepreneurial dreams come to life.

CHAPTER 4

45

GENERATING BUSINESS IDEAS
F

"Business opportunities are like buses, there's always another one coming."
– Richard Branson

inding the right business idea is crucial for entrepreneurial success. This chapter explores various methods for generating and refining business ideas, emphasizing actionable strategies and personal insights.

SKILLS AND TRAINING

Leverage your existing skills and training to start a business. For instance, if you have a degree in accounting, consider offering consultancy services. Skills acquired from previous roles, such as event organization, can also be valuable. Starting with what you know reduces costs and simplifies the process. You can begin by renting equipment and gradually investing in your venture as it grows.

PASSION

Passion is a powerful motivator. It drives you to excel and can be the foundation of a successful business. As Michael Cullinan puts it, "If your passion is business and your business is a passion, you are going to have the love affair of a lifetime." Developing a business around what you love can be highly rewarding. Teresa Collins also highlights the importance of passion: "A successful business requires one simple thing:

PASSION." Consider nurturing your passion with further training to enhance your business potential.

HOBBIES

Turning a hobby into a business can be an effective strategy. Hobbies like photography, cooking, or crafting can evolve into profitable ventures if they become a passion. While hobbies are typically pursued for enjoyment, they can provide a strong foundation for a business. For example, my interest in homemaking led to a successful Airbnb business and further studies in Interior Design. Evaluate your hobbies and explore which ones could be developed into a business.

FRUSTRATIONS

Frustrations often reveal unmet needs in the market. If you encounter a problem, others may be experiencing the same issue. For instance, if there is a lack of barber shops in your area, this could signal a business opportunity. Addressing such gaps by providing the missing product or service can lead to a successful venture. Identifying and solving these problems is key to creating a relevant business.

NECESSITIES

Building a business around necessities ensures a consistent market. Essentials such as food, water, and shelter are always in demand. While focusing on these areas, consider market competition and product differentiation. For example, starting a food business guarantees a customer base, but selecting the right niche and location is crucial. Here are some ways of coming up with a business idea:

SKILLS OR TRAINING

Take a look at what you have learnt as a course, diploma, degree, or any area of specialization. For example, I went for Accounting Consultancy because I studied accounting and have a degree, so I offer a service in my area of training. You can also have a skill that you acquired in your line of work; this means that you do not necessarily qualify, but you gained the skill on the job. For example, you may have worked as an administrator or even a cleaner at a company that coordinates events, and as a result, thereof, you now know how events are organized because you have been helping out with that.

You can use such a skill to start your own business. Using your existing skills or training is an easier and cheaper way of starting a business because you already know, so you become the labor yourself. You can start by hiring equipment from those who have them and set up your business bit by bit. It is much easier if it is technical and does not require equipment (for example, consulting services).

PASSION

As mentioned earlier in the book, passion is an idea that you are passionate about, it drives you, motivates you, and helps you remain consistent. I consider that your passion is usually a gift that you are born with, you don't put too much effort into this. A lot of people have not yet discovered their passion because they have not yet put their mind to it. I know a lot of people without any formal training who do very well in things like décor, catering, sewing, knitting, baking etc. For you to make your passion a business you might still need to nurture it with more training. I love this quote by Michael Cullinan. *"If your passion is business and your business is a passion, you are going to have the love affair of a lifetime."*

Also, a quote from Teresa Collins, *"a successful business requires one simple thing; PASSION".*

Passion is what pushes a doctor who is miserable in his career, to shift gears and start a business in farming where he is far more fulfilled. I never used to understand it before, until I went into business.

Before, I didn't understand what would make someone leave their high-paying profession to pursue something else that is completely different. Now I understand that doing what you love and loving what you do is the key to success. Find your passion and build your business on it. Your passion is your bank, make money whilst enjoying what you do.

HOBBIES

This is an interest that you have, something that you choose to do in your own spare time. It usually helps you to relieve stress and tension, it aids with your relaxation. For example, crafts, dancing, playing chess, writing, cooking and so on. I used to think that a hobby and a passion were the same thing, but I soon figured out that there was a difference.

When you are interested in photography, you can take it as a hobby, and do it whenever you have free time, but when you are so passionate about it you devote most of your time to it and start working as a photographer. In fact, a hobby can become a passion. A hobby is mostly done for fun when you are bored or have extra time, but when you are passionate about something, you constantly want to do it and probably feel like you cannot live without it.A hobby can be turned into a business. Start looking at your hobbies and see which one you can turn into a business. You may have many hobbies but there will always be that one you love the most. My hobby is homemaking; whenever I have time to watch television I watch the Home Channel, and I go to furniture and building stores just to see what is there. I have built my Airbnb business through my hobby and have even gone to get a Diploma in Interior Design out of this hobby which turned into a passion. My passions are home organising, teaching, training, and business empowerment. I cannot do without them, they complete me. I love these deeply and never get tired when I am doing them.

FRUSTRATIONS

If you are frustrated by something, there is a chance that there are other people who share the same frustrations. For example, in the area where you stay there is no barber shop or a saloon, and every time you need that service you travel a distance to get it. That could be an opportunity for you to look at how you can fulfil that need. You might not be a barber or hairdresser, but you can always employ someone to do it for you and start a business out of that. We call this 'spotting a gap'. Close the gap by offering the product or service that is missing. A business is about offering what the market needs and making money out of it.

NECESSITY

Necessities are those things that are necessary, essential, must-have, needed or a requirement. These are food, air, water, and shelter. If you can build your business around offering a necessity, the market will always be there for you. Yes, your success will depend on other factors, but there will always be people who need those things.

If you start selling food, you surely know people will come to buy your items because they cannot do without food, the only element you may have to take into consideration is which type of food you want to sell. Check-in your area, capitalise on the gap you find and start a successful and growing business.

An idea is only an idea until you do something about it. No value when there is no action. Get an idea of what you want to do and do it. The power is in the doing. You can have as many brilliant ideas as possible but if you do not act on them, you are just like the person who does not even know what starting a business is.

THE GAP ANALYSIS

You can also come up with a business idea by identifying a gap in the market using the PESTEL and SWOT analysis. These models are also used in managing your business. When you analyze all the factors involved, you can come up with strategies on how to manage and grow your business.

THE PESTEL MODEL

This model is used to understand the business environment that you will be operating in. Once the risks and opportunities are identified, it leads to better planning. As a business owner, you need to understand how risks should be managed when they arise so that you can come up with a risk management strategy.

Opportunities on the other hand need to be exploited to build a profitable business around or to grow and diversify. This model looks at 6 elements, which we will look into below:

POLITICAL (P)

These determine the extent to which government may influence your business – examples include but are not limited to tax policies and any other policies which may affect trading. If you would like to start a business, you need to check if there is political stability in the country. You cannot do certain businesses where you know the area always has riots and people looting because you will lose everything. Government policies may also be favourable for you to expand your business; for example, favourable import and export policies.

As a business owner, it is crucial to understand all the political factors that can affect your business, whether favourable or unfavourable, to properly plan.

ECONOMIC (E)

These are factors to do with the economy's performance and may either have a negative or positive impact on the sustainability of the business. Such factors include interest rates, inflation, foreign exchange rates and so on. If there is too much inflation, your business will be affected by price fluctuations all the time, which will ultimately influence how you price products and services. If the economy is down and there are job losses, you need to focus on necessities, not luxury goods.

SOCIAL (S)

Social factors look at the people in the area where you want to invest in your business. These factors include demographics, culture, population growth rates etc. For example, you cannot introduce a business that is mainly for young people (e.g., such as trending fashion) in an area where there are mostly old people. Understanding the culture and religion of that area also helps.

There are certain things people don't buy because of religion; for example, in certain places, people don't consume pork and related products. An understanding of the social factors will help you make a good analysis of what you should offer or not and also help you identify which gaps can be capitalised.

TECHNOLOGICAL (T)

These factors pertain to advancements in technology[1] that may affect the operations in a particular market; such factors can either be favourable or unfavourable to your business. They refer to automation, research and development[2], as well as the amount of technological awareness that a market possesses. The level of technological advancement of the target market will help you understand what you need to offer. You cannot go to the village and start a business similar to Uber Eats which uses online processes to function. Obviously, that business will be a failure before it even starts. Most people do not even have smart phones over there, they may also have a problem with stable internet, and most of the people living there may not even afford data.

Before launching a business, look for the technological abilities of your market. If it requires technological advancements, look for a way to work around it so that your service or product offering will be seamless.

ENVIRONMENTAL (E)

---

1.   https://pestleanalysis.com/technological-factors-affecting-business/

2.   https://www.seoreseller.com/#_853ae90f0351324bd73ea615e6487517__4c761f170e016 836ff84498202b99827__853ae90f0351324bd73ea615e6487517_text_43ec3e5dee6e706af776 6fffea512721_Streamline_0bcef9c45bd8a48eda1b26eb0c61c869_20client_0bcef9c45bd8a48e da1b26eb0c61c869_20reporting

Factors around this include the climate, weather, or pollution. Take a look at the laws regarding the environment. Let's just say that you would like to be manufacturing chemicals, what are the policies regarding the disposal of waste? To add, if your business is going to be affected by the climate you need to be sure that where you are located is favourable for that climate or offers something that will work in line with the climate.

LEGAL (L)

An understanding of the law will help you make decisions that align with your business. You need to understand employment laws if you are going to employ staff. You will also need to know consumer laws and the regulatory bodies responsible for your particular business.

For example, if you want to open a canteen or run a bar, there are certain licenses required. It would be sad to start a business and do all the set-up, only for it to be closed down by authorities the next day. The PESTEL analysis will give you an idea of what to offer in the market. It allows you to see gaps and opportunities, and at the same time, it gives you the knowledge of what will work and not work. Having such a clear picture of the environment you are operating in will help you to succeed. Business is all about understanding your market and offering that market what its audience is looking for, not what you want them to buy from you. For any business idea you may have, make sure to use this analysis. You might think that your business idea is wrong, but the PESTEL analysis can reveal that this is not the case; it can show you that what is actually wrong is the market you are operating in.

SWOT ANALYSIS

We are going to look at another key area to take into account for a business to succeed. You should do what is called a SWOT analysis. When you do a SWOT analysis, you are looking at the (internal factors) of your business, the market, your customers or the environment you operate in (external factors).

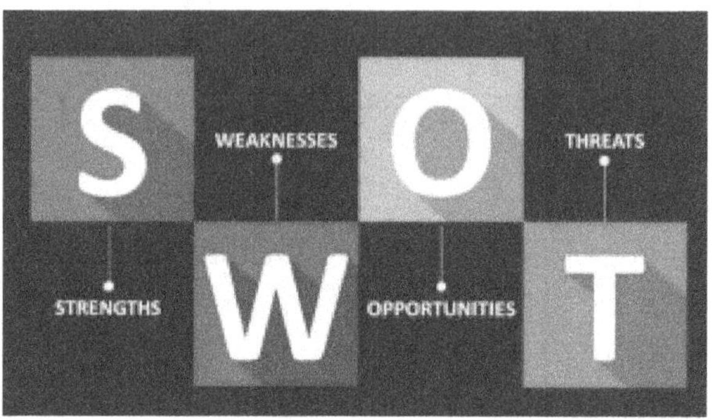

INTERNAL

These we looked at partly in the self-awareness assessment (refer to chapter 1). In business, you need to work on the weaknesses and capitalise on the strengths.

S-Strength

W-Weaknesses

Business weaknesses may include:

Poor business location

Inability to meet demand

Poor customer service

Out-of-date machinery

Out-of-stock problems

Poor technology

Poor financial manageent

If the business has such weaknesses and does not improve, it is only a matter of time before it collapses.

A business may have the following strengths:

Quality products

Good customer service

Efficient and Reliable service

Easy access, good location

Competitive Pricing

Strengths are positives that will make your business succeed and continue to grow. Strengths still need to be monitored because, with the change of staff, for instance, some things might also be affected.

EXTERNAL

These are factors that lie outside the business, they are influenced by the marketplace.

O – opportunities

T – threats

Examples of opportunities are as follows:

Growth of demand

New technology to utilize

Untapped markets

Government assistance or grants

Less competition

Whatever opportunities are there, you can take advantage of them to set up your business or to scale your business going forward. Opportunities create favourable conditions for business.

A few threats to be aware of:

A Suffering economy

Inflation

Competition

Costly regulations

Political instability

Shortage of manpower

Threats work against the growth of businesses, so you need to understand the threats that are present so that your business is not caught by surprise when things are not going well. Plan on how you can manage these threats.

To be a successful entrepreneur you need to put in the work and understand what is going on around you. You always need to change the way you are doing things to continue to be relevant. These models need to be used regularly to monitor any changes in the business environment and act accordingly.

CHAPTER 5

BUILDING CONFIDENCE

"Confidence is not, 'They will like me.' Confidence is, 'I'll be fine if they don't.'" — Christina Grimmie

C onfidence means having faith in your capabilities and decisions. In business, believing in yourself is essential for success. It's not about comparing yourself to others but about embracing your unique strengths and qualities.

HOW TO BECOME CONFIDENT

Stop Comparing Yourself to Others- Comparisons breed self-doubt. Focus on your journey and progress. Recognize that everyone has their own talents and paths. Embrace your uniqueness and strengths. Loving and accepting yourself as you are boosts self-confidence. Don't let others' achievements undermine your self-worth.

Surround Yourself with Positive People- Your environment influences your confidence. Avoid those who belittle or discourage you. Surround yourself with supportive individuals who uplift and motivate you. Positive relationships nurture a confident mindset and encourage personal growth.

Take Care of Yourself- Self-care enhances confidence. Engage in activities that promote well-being, such as exercise, healthy eating, and meditation. Proper rest prevents burnout and supports emotional stability. Grooming and presenting yourself well boost self-esteem and how others perceive you. Looking professional and well-groomed isn't just about vanity—it's about presenting yourself in a way that inspires confidence in others.

Customers are more likely to trust and engage with someone who exudes professionalism.

Treat Yourself Kindly- Mistakes and setbacks are part of business and life. Learn from them without harsh self-criticism. Be compassionate towards yourself, acknowledging that everyone makes mistakes. Viewing setbacks as opportunities for growth rather than failures builds resilience and confidence.

Practice Positive Self-Talk- Monitor your internal dialogue. Replace self-limiting beliefs with affirmations of your capabilities. Avoid phrases like *"I can't"* or *"I'm not good enough."* Instead, affirm yourself with statements like *"I am capable" and "I learn from challenges."* Positive self-talk cultivates a mindset of confidence and optimism. Negative self-talk erodes confidence. Challenge negative thoughts with positive affirmations. Believe in your abilities and strengths. Confidence begins with self-belief and positive reinforcement.

Consistency- Confidence grows with experience. Stay committed to your goals and projects. Continuously learning and improving builds competence and self-assurance.

Avoid jumping from one idea to another without seeing it through. Persistence and consistency breed confidence.

Acknowledge Your Achievements- Celebrate your successes, no matter how small. Recognize your efforts and progress. Self-validation boosts confidence, reinforcing your capabilities. Don't rely on external validation; be your own cheerleader.

Understand Your Business- Confidence in business comes from knowing your products or services inside out. Understand their benefits and unique selling points. Confidence in your offerings inspires trust and credibility among customers. Familiarize yourself with customer needs and industry trends to confidently address inquiries and challenges.

Practice Your Pitch- Master presenting your business to potential clients. Prepare for common questions and objections. Enhance your communication skills through practice and feedback. Confidence in presenting your ideas persuades others of your expertise and capability.

Presentations don't have to be perfect; they need to be confident. Embrace imperfections as part of the learning process. Practice and exposure improve presentation skills over time.

THE BENEFITS OF CONFIDENCE

Sense of Achievement: Confidence fuels a sense of accomplishment and progress.

Positivity: Optimism and confidence go hand in hand, fostering a positive mindset.

Motivation: Confidence drives ambition and determination to overcome challenges.

Resilience: Confident individuals bounce back stronger from setbacks.

Reduced Fear and Anxiety: Confidence diminishes apprehension, promoting bold decision-making.

Confidence is fundamental to entrepreneurial success. It underpins your ability to lead, innovate, and thrive in competitive markets. Cultivate confidence through self-awareness, positive reinforcement, and continuous learning.

CHAPTER 6

63

MARKETING

T

In the bustling marketplace of the modern world, marketing is the heartbeat that keeps a business alive. But what exactly is marketing? At its core, marketing is the art and science of creating, communicating, delivering, and exchanging offerings that have value for customers, clients, partners, and society.

It encompasses all activities aimed at promoting and selling products or services, including market research, advertising, and building strong customer relationships.

THE HISTORY OF MARKETING

Marketing is not new; it has evolved significantly over centuries, adapting to societal changes and technological advancements.

Pre-Industrial Revolution

Imagine a time when bartering was the primary means of trade. Craftsmen and traders relied on word of mouth and simple signage to promote their wares. Marketing was personal and direct, often conducted in bustling marketplaces where reputation was everything.

Industrial Revolution (18th-19th Century)

The world changed as mass production emerged. Suddenly, businesses needed to differentiate their products amidst growing competition. This era saw the birth of the first advertising agencies, focusing on print media such as newspapers and magazines.

20thC

The early 20th century witnessed the rise of brand management and market segmentation. The advent of radio and television introduced new advertising channels, revolutionizing how businesses reached their audiences. E. Jerome McCarthy's concept of the "marketing mix" (Product, Price, Place, Promotion) became a cornerstone of modern marketing strategy.

Late 20th - Early 21stC

The digital revolution transformed the marketing landscape once again. The internet, social media, and e-commerce opened up new frontiers, allowing businesses to reach global audiences with unprecedented precision. Data analytics and customer relationship management (CRM) systems enabled businesses to understand and serve their customers better than ever before.

In the 4th Industrial Revolution (4IR), we discovered our lag in marketing, packaging, payment packages, point of sale, and recording stock in books. Adapting to the times, online business gained momentum. We upgraded from plastic bags to gift bags, enhanced staff appearance with uniforms, and communicated with customers outside South Africa.

WHY IS MARKETING IMPORTANT?

- ◈ It spreads your name
- ◈ It boosts your sales
- ◈ It enhances your reputation

◈It helps you gain and retain customers.

The straightforward definition of marketing is any action taken to bring attention to your business. Before you even start marketing, you need to come up with a name for your business. You cannot say I am the cake seller, water seller, or vegetable seller. It sounds better if you say I am from Divine Cakes, I am from Healthy Veges, there is some identity. People remember names better than the person who is offering the service or the product.

HOW TO COME UP WITH A NAME FOR YOUR BUSINESS

Avoid names that are hard to spell.

Make it easy for people to search for your company or to pronounce it.

Do not pick a name that limits you

Have a growth mind-set; for example, Amazon does a lot of selling. Now imagine if it had just limited its name to "Amazon online books", it was going to be limited to one item only.

Do not limit yourself to your geographical area either, for example, by calling yourself "Midrand Clothing", do not put a place as part of the name if you are going to have a wide variety of markets.

Have a name that conveys your speciality

Immediately someone will know what you are doing e.g. Divine Cakes, it says that the person's business is into making cakes.

A catchy name

Come up with something catchy e.g., Trendz. There are some very boring names which do not go together with the target market.

It should sound good

A good name should both look good on paper and sound good to the ears of customers.

Love it yourself

You should love the name of your business; you will be using it more than anyone else. It should speak to you. When you have a name that you want to call your business, test run it with your friends and get their views about it before you start printing all your marketing fliers.

CORPORATE COLORS

After a name, you need to come up with your business colours which are also called corporate colours. Whatever marketing material you are going to do for your business, should have those colours. This is what we call your corporate identity.

Some people use different colours on their fliers all the time, sometimes there is purple and white, sometimes green and orange, and sometimes blue and grey. The reason why people do that is because they do not have this knowledge. Your business colours should be maintained all the time, yes you can change when you want to rebrand, but even afterwards you must maintain what you have changed. Let us look at some of the companies we know like ***FNB, KFC, Capitec Bank, Mr Price etc.***

They have their corporate colours, if you check now, you will see that all their fliers, the décor inside their stores, their adverts, and their uniforms all have those colours. Whenever you go into a shop, try to figure out their corporate colours.

Here is a guide for you to choose your colours based on their meaning. Do not just choose any colour, it should be in line with what you do. Do not put too many colours together either. If you maintain it at three colours that will be great. Lastly, choose your colours based on the purpose of your business. It will not look nice, nor will it make sense for someone doing farming to use the colour pink, but shades of green will have a better impact.

MEANINGS OF CORPORATE COLOURS

Choosing the right colors for your business can significantly impact how your brand is perceived by customers. Colors evoke emotions and associations that can influence purchasing decisions and brand loyalty. Here's a guide to understanding the meanings of various corporate colors:

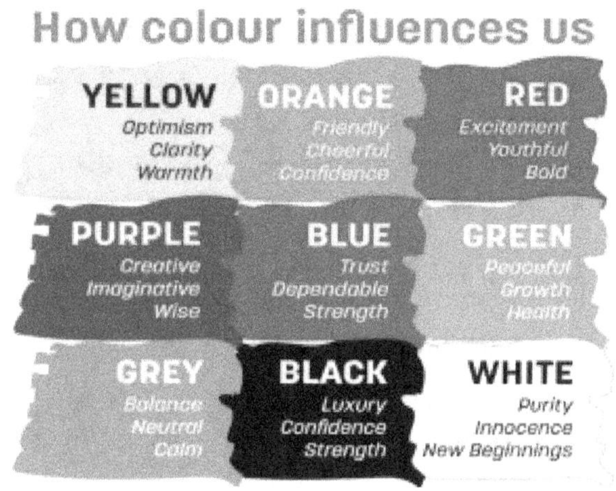

THE POWER OF COLOR IN BRANDING

RED: Power, Passion, Excitement, Anger

Usage: Red is a dynamic, attention-grabbing color that stimulates strong emotions. It signifies urgency and creates a sense of excitement and energy.

- **Examples:**

Coca-Cola: The vibrant red logo evokes feelings of happiness and excitement.

KFC: Red in KFC's branding signifies passion and excitement for their food offerings.

LIGHT BLUE: Tranquility, Trust, Openness

Usage: Light blue is calming and associated with trust and reliability. It's often used by healthcare and financial services companies to convey security and dependability.

- **Examples:**

Twitter: Uses light blue to represent open communication and trust.

Facebook: The light blue shade conveys approachability and reliability.

DARK BLUE: Professionalism, Security, Formality

Usage: Dark blue exudes professionalism and is commonly used by corporate and government organizations to convey stability and authority.

- **Examples:**

IBM: The dark blue in IBM's logo represents professionalism and trustworthiness.

JP Morgan: Uses dark blue to communicate stability and confidence in their financial services.

PINK: Femininity, Youth, Innocence

Usage: Pink is associated with products and services targeted toward women and girls. It conveys softness, care, and nurturing.

- **Examples:**

Victoria's Secret: Utilizes pink to appeal to its primarily female audience, evoking feelings of romance and femininity.

Barbie: The iconic pink color represents youthfulness and playfulness.

YELLOW: Happiness, Youth, Optimism

Usage: Yellow is bright and energizing. It grabs attention and is associated with positive energy and optimism.

- **Examples:**

McDonald's: Uses yellow to evoke feelings of happiness and joy.

IKEA: The yellow in IKEA's branding conveys friendliness and approachability.

GREEN: Health, Environment, Goodwill, Wealth

Usage: Green is connected to nature and is commonly used by brands promoting health, wellness, and eco-friendliness. It also symbolizes growth and prosperity.

- **Examples:**

Starbucks: The green logo represents the company's commitment to sustainability and nature.

Whole Foods: Uses green to emphasize their focus on natural and organic products.

PURPLE: Royalty, Creativity, Luxury

Usage: Purple is associated with luxury, creativity, and imagination. It conveys a sense of premium quality and exclusivity.

- **Examples:**

Cadbury: The purple in Cadbury's branding signifies premium quality and indulgence.

Hallmark: Uses purple to evoke a sense of creativity and luxury in their products.

GOLD: Wealth, Pedigree

Usage: Gold is synonymous with wealth and high status. It's often used by luxury brands and products to convey exclusivity and sophistication.

- **Examples:**

Rolex: Incorporates gold to emphasize luxury and high status.
Louis Vuitton: Uses gold to represent premium quality and exclusivity.

BROWN: Comfort, Relaxation

Usage: Brown is earthy and conveys reliability and comfort. It evokes a sense of warmth and stability.

- **Examples:**

UPS: The brown color in UPS's branding represents reliability and groundedness.

Hershey's: Uses brown to evoke the rich, comforting nature of chocolate.

BLACK: Power, Luxury, Sophistication
Usage: Black is elegant and sophisticated. It conveys luxury, power, and timelessness.

- **Examples:**

Chanel: The black logo is synonymous with sophistication and timeless elegance.

Nike: Uses black to represent strength and sleekness.

ORANGE: Energy, Innovation
Usage: Orange is vibrant and energetic. It helps brands stand out and be seen as innovative and fun.

- **Examples:**

Fanta: Uses orange to evoke fun and energy, fitting for a soda brand.

Home Depot: The orange color represents creativity and enthusiasm in home improvement.

Incorporating these colors thoughtfully into your branding can help convey the right message to your audience and create a lasting impression.

WHAT IS A LOGO?

A logo is a symbol or design used to identify a company.
A good logo should be:
1. *Simple*
2. *Incorporate your company colours*
3. *Balanced*
4. *Relevant to your industry*

5. Pleasing to the eye

Here is an example of the FNB logo.

Their corporate colours are green, gold, and black, and they are well incorporated into the logo. They used green as the colour of money and wealth, gold to symbolise wealth and pedigree and black to evoke that powerful, luxurious feeling to tie the logo together.

PAYOFF LINE

- *It is a branding slogan.*
- *Describe how you do it – create a memorable phrase.*
- *It is a selling point.*
- *It tells why customers should choose you – and reinforces the audience's memory of your service.*

e.g. Ngoho Accounting – *we don't just do numbers we add value.*
Other Examples of payoff lines

- KFC – *it's finger-licking good.*
- McDonald's – *I'm loving it.*
- Nike – *just do it.*
- Coca-Cola – *open happiness*
- FNB – *how can we help you?*

Come up with a branding slogan for your business that describes how you do it, and the value proposition which can reinforce the audience's memory of your service. All this forms part of your brand identity.

MARKETING LITERATURE

Marketing literature encompasses various materials used to promote and communicate about a business. These tools are essential in conveying the business's identity, offerings, and value propositions to potential and existing customers.These are tools that help you communicate with your customers; they give them information about you.

Here are a few examples below:

Business cards

Fliers

A business profile

Brochures

Letterheads

When you do your marketing literature, incorporate everything we have discussed above. The name, the corporate colours, the logo, and the payoff line. Your literature should answer the following questions to the customer;

Who are you?

Customers should not ask you for your company name, it should be clear.

What do you do?

The business products should be clear, what you supply or services you give. Pictures will be ideal if they are products.

Who do i contact & how to contact you?

Your name should be there as the person to be contacted. You need to have the telephone number, WhatsApp number and or email address.

Where do we find you?

You should put your address, and where you are operating from so that if someone wants to come to your store, people know where you are based.

Where can we see more?

These are your social media pages, your website and anything else that shows clients where they can see or learn more about your business. Everyone running a business should always have their business cards or fliers with them. These are the tools of trade. It is easier to just give someone a flier than to start explaining everything and even say, *"Do you have pen and paper to write my number?"*Here is an example of a flier. This is the flier for Ngoho Accounting and Business Consultants combining all the elements we discussed, logo, payoff line, corporate colors, and all the info that should be provided.

CHANNELS TO USE FOR MARKETING?

You are the best channel for marketing your business.

Approach people and talk about your business, any opportunity you get at church, gatherings, the mall etc., present your products, **SELL**. Word of mouth is the best kind of marketing because you can explain more and give more information which can then persuade someone to buy your product or use your service. Instead of gossiping, tell them about your business.

The easiest one is also your WhatsApp status

Your status should mostly be about your business, people should know what you do via your WhatsApp status. Have nice pictures of what you sell and advertise them there.

Furthermore, avoid sharing 20 pics at once, people won't even look at all of them, just 3 or 4 a day.

WhatsApp groups

Create a group where you can advertise your products; also share on other WhatsApp groups you have not created, if they allow advertising.

Facebook page

This is becoming the most popular channel of advertising, there are so many people on Facebook who can be your clients. The best is when you promote the page and also FB advertising which you pay for. Beware of scammers on social media though.

Instagram, TikTok, YouTube

All these are some of the social media channels which can be utilized for marketing. Learn how these are used for marketing and start doing what you can.

Website

A website is also a marketing tool because people will be able to find all the information they need and also, and you can sell via your website - this is called e-commerce.

It is advisable to get a good graphic designer who can make nice fliers and business cards for you. This person or company can help you with your logo, putting your corporate colours together and others also print for you. It will be a one-stop shop. Good quality material sells on its own, and mostly this is a once-off cost, you don't change your branding every time.

I am still using the same logo and colors from when I started. This is the promotion part/aspect of marketing. You need to promote your products and make noise about them, otherwise, no one will know and if nobody knows you exist, there is no business.

THE PRODUCT

Another element of marketing is looking at the product itself or the service you are offering. This is what makes or breaks the business, what you are selling is the ***BUSINESS.***

Components of a good product
Function

The product should be able to fulfill its purpose. For example, washing powder can only be regarded as good if it has foam and has the strength to remove dirt.

Quality

This is measured by durability. If the product is not durable, it is a poor product. For example, if you buy a dress you wash it once and all the seams are out.

People argue that the quality you get depends on the price you pay. It is true, but the quality should still be acceptable even if the price is affordable.

Packaging

The packaging should be attractive for customers to at least want to try your product out. This is where proper branding comes in. If you just package your product in a black packet no one will look twice, but if you use some bright colours people will want to see more. Go into a store and at look how the products are packaged, everyone competes on the use of colour.

The quality of the packaging itself matters; some people use cheap packaging that breaks as soon as the client holds it. Packaging also touches the handling of the product, imagine if the 10kg mealie meal bag didn't have a handle, it would be difficult to carry. Another example is if you bake cakes, you need to have boxes to package them nicely for easy handling, unlike using a plastic bag.

Ease of use

The product should not be so complicated to use. If it is a complex product have a clear and easy-to-use manual. No matter how good your product is, if it is complicated, people will not buy it. Whatever product you sell, must indicate that you understand your customers.

Ask yourself these questions:
What do they want?
What kind of products do they want to buy?
How do they want it?
In what sizes, colours etc.?
How much do they want it for?
What can they afford to pay?
How easy can they buy it?
Are they able to buy online or do they want a physical store and in which location?

SERVICES

For those who sell services, it is much harder for you because the customer cannot see or feel it like a product, they are buying an experience. They can only buy based on the benefits offered, more than features. These are factors such as consultancy services, hospitality, massages , and so on. If you are in this industry, what also sells is the customer confidence in you, you have to learn how to pitch right.

PLACE/LOCATION

People always want convenience when they do their shopping. If you are going to have a physical shop, make sure it is easy for customers to find and get there. There should be a good transport network and good roads for easy accessibility. If you are selling heavy goods, you cannot be on the top floor and there are no lifts, which will discourage your customers from coming to your shop. The location of business is not only physical, nowadays we do a lot of business online, if you do online business make sure the website is easy to use, secure and functioning – not always offline.

This aspect also looks at the delivery of the items to customers, if you have a delivery facility make sure that it is reliable. If you give a delivery date and time to a customer, that should be adhered to. If not, it will be a great inconvenience that can make you lose business. Problems happen yes, so if you know you cannot deliver on the specified date and time, talk to the client beforehand. Do not to wait for the client to call you to follow up on their delivery. Exceptional customer service is always key in business; under promise and overdeliver not the other way around.

Let us look at some marketing dos and don'ts that can help you do well in marketing your business;

MARKETING DO'S AND DON'TS

Don'ts

1. Don't post a pic with no price, no description, nothing. When people ask how much, don't just randomly put the number 30 (30 what? Rands? Dollars).Or worse, using the phrase, 'Inbox for more info'. Why sell your products like you are selling drugs?

2. If someone asks, "Who sells e.g., soap" and you answer, "Me!" or even worse just put an emoji of a raised hand, that's it.

No explanation e.g., where you are, how much your products are worth, your contact number etc.

3. Don't apologise for what your product is offering. "I am so sorry my products are a bit expensive" Why would you do that? As a customer, I would not buy it because you are showing me that it's not good enough. That's what you are conveying when you apologise about your product.

4. Don't say, I am selling a *'No Name'.* What's that? Will customers remember that?

5. When people ask about your product you are either very defensive or even abusive, using responses like *"Well I didn't force you to buy, did I"* Really? What happened to... *"The customer is always right?"...*You need to keep this GOLDEN RULE in mind.

6. Non-approachability...

MARKETING MUST DO'S

1. Good descriptions/prices/contact details (including country code on your phone numbers) with every product you post.

Don't wait for your customers to ask, that will be your loss.

2. People buy from people...not just products (food for thought). Introduce yourself, and state your full name. Don't post the same monotonous advert to the same audience daily. Be creative. Share product knowledge.

3. Be professional, dress well. Yes, check yourself in the mirror and ask yourself, 'Would I buy from me?'

4. Address people well e.g., don't call your customer dear, love, darling... that's not professional, too personal... it's wrong. Call them sir/madam or respectfully use their names if you know them.

5. Use good English. Even if it might not be your first language, there is no excuse for not improving. Also, never use slang.

6. Know your products. Or find the information for your customers. Go that extra mile.

7. Your passion for your product/business will get you, customers.

8. Make your customer feel important.

9. Offer incentives e.g., if you are a hairdresser, give 10% off to your first-time customer, or give 10% off their next appointment if they introduce you to another customer.

If you are selling a handbag, maybe you can say: 'this handbag is R25; I will throw in a pair of glasses for you.'

10. USP (Unique Selling Point)

What's special about your product? E.g., 20 other ladies are selling the same handbag WHY should I buy yours?

11. Use as many marketing platforms as you can. There are many free platforms you can utilise (gone are the days when people used Facebook for gossip... people are making millions on Facebook, so jump on it).

If you are making R10 today aim to make R20 tomorrow. Grow your business and expand it.

Author ~ Unknown

Price
is what you pay.
Value
is what you get.

Warren Buffett

CHAPTER 8

83

PRICING

Pricing is one of the most critical aspects of any business strategy. It is the art and science of determining what a company will receive in exchange for its products or services. While often considered merely a matter of setting prices, effective pricing strategies involve understanding market conditions, consumer behavior, and the overall economic environment.

Pricing also refers to the process of setting a value or monetary amount for a product or service that a customer is willing to pay. It is a critical element of the marketing mix (alongside product, place, and promotion) and directly impacts a company's profitability, market positioning, and customer perceptions. Pricing is the process of determining what a company will charge for its products or services. This process involves more than simply deciding a number; it encompasses various factors such as cost of production, market demand, competitive landscape, and perceived value. A well-defined pricing strategy can help a business achieve its financial goals, attract and retain customers, and maintain a competitive edge.

The concept of pricing has evolved significantly over centuries. In ancient times, the barter system was the primary means of exchange, where goods and services were traded directly.

As economies grew more complex, the need for a common medium of exchange led to the development of money, and with it, the concept of price as we know it today.

Medieval Times: In medieval Europe, the price of goods was often determined by local guilds and regulated by the government. Prices were set to ensure fairness and prevent exploitation.

Industrial Revolution: The Industrial Revolution brought about mass production, which necessitated new pricing strategies. Businesses began to consider production costs, competition, and consumer demand more systematically.

20th Century: The 20th century saw the rise of various pricing models and theories, including cost-plus pricing, value-based pricing, and dynamic pricing. The advent of technology and globalization further influenced pricing strategies, making them more complex and data-driven.

PRICING STRATEGIES AND THEIR IMPACT

Different pricing strategies can significantly impact a business's success. Here are some common strategies and their implications:

1. Cost-Plus Pricing: This straightforward method involves adding a fixed percentage to the cost of producing a product. While simple, it doesn't consider market demand or competitor pricing.

2. Value-Based Pricing: This strategy sets prices based on the perceived value to the customer rather than the cost of production. It requires a deep understanding of the target market and can lead to higher profit margins.

3. Competitive Pricing: Businesses set prices based on what competitors are charging. This strategy is common in highly competitive markets and can help attract price-sensitive customers.

4. Penetration Pricing: Used to enter a new market, penetration pricing sets a low price to attract customers quickly. Once a customer base is established, prices are gradually increased.

5. Skimming Pricing: This involves setting high prices initially to target customers willing to pay a premium. Prices are lowered over time to attract a broader audience. This strategy is often used for innovative or high-tech products.

6. Dynamic Pricing: Prices are adjusted in real-time based on demand, supply, and other market factors. This approach is common in industries like airlines and hospitality.

THE PSYCHOLOGICAL IMPACT OF PRICING

Pricing isn't just about economics; it also has a psychological component. How a price is presented can influence consumer perception and behavior.

1. Price Anchoring: The first price a customer sees can set a reference point for what they're willing to pay. For instance, showing a higher-priced item first can make subsequent items seem more affordable.

2. Charm Pricing: Ending prices in .99 or .95 can make them appear significantly lower than a rounded number, even if the difference is minimal.

3. Price Bundling: Offering products or services together at a lower combined price can encourage customers to purchase more than they originally intended.

THE FUTURE OF PRICING

As technology continues to advance, pricing strategies are becoming more sophisticated. Big data and artificial intelligence enable businesses to analyze vast amounts of information and set prices with unprecedented precision. Additionally, the rise of e-commerce and global marketplaces means businesses must be more agile and responsive to international pricing trends and consumer preferences. Technological advancements are making pricing strategies more sophisticated. Big data and AI enable precise pricing based on vast amounts of information. E-commerce and global marketplaces require agility in pricing to respond to international trends and preferences.

Pricing is a dynamic and multifaceted aspect of business strategy. From its origins in ancient barter systems to the complex, data-driven approaches of today, pricing has always played a crucial role in economic exchange. By understanding the various strategies and their psychological impacts, businesses can set prices that attract customers, maximize profits, and ensure long-term success. Pricing is a dynamic and multifaceted aspect of business strategy.

From its origins in ancient barter systems to the complex, data-driven approaches of today, pricing has always played a crucial role in economic exchange. By understanding various strategies and their psychological impacts, businesses can set prices that attract customers, maximize profits, and ensure long-term success.

CHAPTER 9

BUSINESS FINANCES

The goal isn't more money. The goal is living life on your terms." — Chris Brogan

N

ow that your business is generating revenue, effective financial management becomes crucial. Businesses often fail due to poor financial discipline and mismanagement of funds. To ensure long-term success and growth, it's essential to implement sound financial practices from the outset.

THE IMPORTANCE OF FINANCIAL DISCIPLINE

Financial discipline is the cornerstone of sustainable business growth. Many entrepreneurs struggle because they spend all their capital without planning for future expenses or growth. Here's how you can manage your finances effectively:

Separate Personal and Business Finances: Open separate accounts for your personal and business finances. Pay yourself a salary from the business account and strictly adhere to this division. This separation helps in tracking business expenses accurately and prevents personal spending from affecting business operations.

Avoid Cash Transactions: Instead of dealing in cash, encourage customers to pay electronically or deposit cash into your business account. Cash is easy to spend without accountability, whereas electronic transactions provide a clear record for budgeting and financial planning.

Reinvest Profits: Resist the temptation to spend all profits on personal expenses. Reinvesting profits back into the business fuels growth.

Allocate funds towards larger orders, improved equipment, enhanced marketing efforts, staff training, and technological advancements. This strategic reinvestment ensures continuous improvement and competitiveness in the market.

Create and Follow a Budget: Develop a comprehensive budget that outlines expected income and expenses. Stick to this budget rigorously to avoid overspending or unnecessary purchases. Budgeting is a skill that improves with practice and helps in managing cash flow effectively.

Prefer Cash Transactions: Conduct business on a cash basis whenever possible. This approach maintains a healthy cash flow and reduces the risk of bad debt. If extending credit is necessary, ensure strict credit control measures to minimize outstanding debts and accelerate cash inflows.

Maintain Accurate Records: Keep detailed records of all financial transactions, including sales, expenses, and investments. Regularly review these records to track profitability, identify trends, and make informed financial decisions.

Utilize basic accounting tools like Excel initially and consider upgrading to specialized software or hiring a professional bookkeeper as your business grows.

Effective financial management requires discipline, foresight, and a commitment to long-term business sustainability. By prioritizing financial stability and growth, you lay a solid foundation for achieving your business goals and weathering economic challenges.

CHAPTER 10

KEY AREAS OF SUCCESS

"Success in business requires training, discipline, and hard work. But if you're not frightened by these things, the opportunities are just as great today as they ever were." — David Rockefeller

W

e are going to look in summary at the key areas to building a profitable business. We have covered them in the previous chapters, but we will revise them together: In this chapter, we will summarize the key areas essential for building a profitable business.

Each of these areas has been discussed in detail in previous chapters, but here we will revisit and consolidate their importance together.

THE ENTREPRENEURIAL MINDSET

The entrepreneurial mindset encompasses a set of attitudes, behaviors, and skills that drive individuals to identify opportunities, take calculated risks, innovate, and persevere in the face of challenges. It is a critical factor in the success of entrepreneurs and their ventures. Building a successful business starts with cultivating the right mindset. Here are key attributes to foster:

*Positivity***:** Maintain an optimistic outlook to overcome challenges and believe in positive outcomes. A positive mindset is crucial for resilience and enduring success in business.

Self-Motivation: Internal drive is vital for sustaining momentum. Be your own motivator and pursue your goals with determination, regardless of external validation.

Creativity: Think innovatively to solve problems and meet market needs. Embrace fresh ideas and approaches to differentiate your business.

Tenacity: Persevere through setbacks and challenges. Business success often hinges on resilience and the ability to bounce back stronger.

Flexibility: Adapt quickly to changing circumstances and market conditions. Being flexible allows you to seize opportunities and navigate obstacles effectively.

Passion: Infuse enthusiasm into your business endeavors. Genuine passion attracts customers and inspires loyalty.

Receptivity: Remain open to new ideas and feedback. Listening to others fosters growth and innovation within your business.

MARKETING

As previously discussed, effective marketing is essential for business visibility and growth. Without marketing, your business remains invisible to potential customers.

CUSTOMER SERVICE

Exceptional customer service is non-negotiable for business success. Providing a memorable customer experience fosters loyalty and distinguishes your brand from competitors.

*High-Quality Service***:** Ensure every customer interaction exceeds expectations. Superior service builds trust and encourages repeat business.

Prompt Feedback: Respond promptly to inquiries and address customer concerns promptly. Follow up after sales to gauge satisfaction and gather feedback.

Integrity: Uphold honesty and reliability in all business dealings. Transparency enhances credibility and customer trust.

EFFICIENCY

Operational efficiency enhances productivity and profitability:

Cost Management: Strive for cost-efficiency without compromising quality. Negotiate discounts with suppliers and optimize production processes to reduce waste.

Quality Control: Maintain high standards in product or service delivery. Consistent quality builds reputation and customer satisfaction.

Speed and Reliability: Ensure timely delivery and responsiveness. Reliable service strengthens customer relationships and business reputation.

CASH FLOW MANAGEMENT

Effective cash flow management is crucial for business sustainability:

Positive Cash Flow: Ensure income exceeds expenses to avoid reliance on debt. Monitor cash flow regularly and maintain accurate financial records.

Budgeting: Develop and adhere to a budget to control spending and allocate resources effectively. Understanding your financial position is key to making informed decisions.

CONTINUOUS IMPROVEMENT

Business success requires ongoing learning and adaptation:

Learning Culture: Embrace continuous learning through courses, webinars, and mentorship. Invest in your knowledge to stay ahead of industry trends.

Adaptation: Continuously refine business strategies, systems, and customer service based on feedback and market changes. Flexibility and adaptation ensure long-term relevance and growth.

Incorporate these key areas into your business strategy to foster growth, profitability, and long-term success. Each element plays a crucial role in building a resilient and competitive business in today's dynamic marketplace.

CHOOSING THE RIGHT BUSINESS

Selecting the right business to start is a critical decision that requires careful consideration. Here are some steps to guide you:

1. **Self-Assessment:**

Passions and Interests: Identify what you are passionate about. A business aligned with your interests is more likely to keep you motivated and engaged.

Skills and Expertise: Assess your skills and experiences. Choose a business that leverages your strengths or areas where you have significant expertise.

1. **Market Research:**

Identify Needs: Look for gaps in the market or problems that need solving. A successful business often addresses a specific need or demand.

Analyze Competition: Research existing competitors. Understanding their strengths and weaknesses can help you find a unique angle or niche for your business.

1. **Feasibility Study:**

Cost and Resources: Evaluate the initial investment required and the resources available to you. Ensure you have or can acquire the necessary resources to start and sustain the business.

Profitability: Estimate potential revenue and expenses to assess the business's financial viability.

1. **Customer Validation:**

Feedback: Seek feedback from potential customers to gauge interest and willingness to pay for your product or service.

Pilot Testing: Consider running a pilot or test version of your business to gather real-world insights and refine your approach.

1. **Long-Term Vision:**

Sustainability: Think about the long-term prospects of the business. Ensure it has the potential for growth and scalability.

Alignment with Goals: Ensure the business aligns with your personal and professional goals. It should fit within your broader vision for your life and career.

CONCLUSION

B

uilding a business is much like constructing a house—from laying the foundation to adding the finishing touches, and then maintaining it over time. Just as a house requires ongoing upkeep, so does your business. You start with a solid foundation, refine your strategies, and continually improve to increase profitability.

Whether you're just beginning your entrepreneurial journey or you've been in business for years, learning is constant. It's a journey, not a destination—a path of continuous growth and adaptation.

If you haven't started yet, I encourage you to begin today. It won't always be easy, but with dedication and the right mindset, it can be an incredibly rewarding experience. Don't wait for the perfect moment; seize the opportunity now. As Carrie Fisher once said, *"Stay afraid, but do it anyway."* Action is what matters most.Ignore the naysayers and doubters. People will always find reasons to criticize, but confidence in yourself and your vision is key.

Embrace challenges as lessons, not failures. Learn from mistakes, adjust, and keep moving forward. I, too, was once fearful of starting my business. Looking back, I realize my fears were unfounded. Fear is overrated; courage and persistence are what count. Entrepreneurship demands resilience and determination. It's about taking consistent steps toward your goals, knowing that success takes time.

Remember, every setback is a stepping stone to success. Invest in learning, seek mentorship, and use your time wisely. Surround yourself with like-minded individuals who inspire and challenge you. Business is both challenging and exhilarating—fuel your journey with passion and a relentless pursuit of excellence.

Thank you for joining me on this journey through my book. Watch out for my future publications, expanding on the insights we've explored here. You have everything you need to succeed in building and running a profitable business. Believe in yourself and your abilities. You are worthy of success.

Until next time...

GLOSSARY

- **Ambidextrous Organizations**: Organizations capable of managing both evolutionary and revolutionary change simultaneously.
- **Budgeting**: The process of creating a plan to spend your money, ensuring you have enough resources for essential expenditures and savings.
- **Cash Flow Management**: Monitoring, analyzing, and optimizing the net amount of cash receipts minus cash expenses.
- **Credit Control**: Measures to ensure that customers pay their invoices within the credit terms agreed upon.
- **Customer Service**: The assistance and advice provided by a company to those people who buy or use its products or services.
- **Entrepreneurial Mindset**: A set of attitudes, behaviors, and skills that drive individuals to identify opportunities, take calculated risks, innovate, and persevere in the face of challenges.
- **Financial Discipline**: The practice of managing finances with a strategic and controlled approach to ensure long-term sustainability and growth.
- **Marketing**: The action or business of promoting and selling products or services, including market research and advertising.
- **Operational Efficiency**: The ability of an organization to deliver products or services in the most cost-effective manner without sacrificing quality.
- **Reinvestment**: The action of investing profits back into the

business to fuel growth and expansion.

BIBLIOGRAPHY

- Goleman, D. (1995). *Emotional Intelligence: Why It Can Matter More Than IQ*. Bantam Books.
- Pink, D. H. (2009). *Drive: The Surprising Truth About What Motivates Us*. Riverhead Books.
- Csikszentmihalyi, M. (1990). *Flow: The Psychology of Optimal Experience*. Harper & Row.
- Cohen, S., & Wills, T. A. (1985). Stress, social support, and the buffering hypothesis. *Psychological Bulletin, 98*(2), 310-357.
- Fredrickson, B. L. (2001). The role of positive emotions in positive psychology: The broaden-and-build theory of positive emotions. *American Psychologist, 56*(3), 218-226.
- Snyder, C. R. (2002). Hope theory: Rainbows in the mind. *Psychological Inquiry, 13*(4), 249-275.
- Tushman, M. L., & O'Reilly, C. A. (1996). Ambidextrous organizations: Managing evolutionary and revolutionary change. *California Management Review, 38*(4), 8-30.
- Brown, C., & Petersen, M. (2015). *The Entrepreneur's Guide to Business Success*. Business Press.
- Hisrich, R. D., Peters, M. P., & Shepherd, D. A. (2017). *Entrepreneurship*. McGraw-Hill Education.

Don't miss out!

Visit the website below and you can sign up to receive emails whenever Munyaradzi Gumbo-Mberi publishes a new book. There's no charge and no obligation.

https://books2read.com/r/B-A-RXARB-HHJVD

Connecting independent readers to independent writers.

About the Author

Known affectionately as "Munya," she wears many hats, excelling as a Chartered Certified Accountant, Motivational Speaker, Business Coach, and successful entrepreneur. Munya is a dynamic catalyst for empowerment, dedicated to inspiring individuals to embark on their entrepreneurial journeys and achieve remarkable success. Her passion lies in motivating people to start and thrive in their businesses. As a business coach, Munya transcends conventional guidance, embedding the powerful belief that business success is not a distant dream but a tangible reality. Her mantra is clear: It is doable. It is achievable. It is possible. This book distills the essence of the courses she teaches, tailored for startups and those aspiring to elevate their businesses. Through her multifaceted expertise and unwavering dedication, Munya aims to equip aspiring entrepreneurs with the tools, strategies, and mindset necessary to navigate the complexities of the business world and achieve their fullest potential.

www.ingramcontent.com/pod-product-compliance
Lightning Source LLC
Chambersburg PA
CBHW071349150726
47997CB00002B/921